A WALKER IN THE CITY

A WALKER IN THE CITY

Méira Cook

Brick Books

Library and Archives Canada Cataloguing in Publication

Cook, Méira, 1964-
    A walker in the city / Méira Cook.

Poems.
ISBN 978-1-926829-72-2

    I. Title.

PS8555.O567W35 2011   C811'.54   C2011-904257-6

We acknowledge the Canada Council for the Arts, the Government of
Canada through the Canada Book Fund, and the Ontario Arts Council
for their support of our publishing program.

Cover design by Cheryl Dipede.

The author photo was taken by Mark Libin.

The book is set in Minion and Akzidenz Grostesk.

Design and layout by Alan Siu.

Printed and bound by Sunville Printco Inc.

Brick Books
431 Boler Road, Box 20081
London, Ontario N6K 4G6

www.brickbooks.ca

For my loves —

Mark and Shoshana
and
Misha and Shai

Contents

A Walker in the City

Where to send her, this walker?

Go little mine book. She sets off
coat swinging wide. Stars
in her wake and moons in theirs
collide.

— from *Loitering With Intent*
 by F. Kulperstein

Astringent day in early winter
when all the angels have been let out
of their cages. The wet blue beak
of morning, sky skidding on ahead

or flying — the sky — *flying* laundry.
Shunting cirrus back and forth (sky)
swerving its tracks boing-boing,
rubber as a ball highing

the bluest bit of hush at the centre
of a jaunty girl's jaunty eye.
Callooh! Callay! arias she out (but soft
away). Then, shining all

and sure, vaults she the wind's
cathedral, stamping booted feet,
lifting a hand unmittened, yes,
the better to balance welterweight

wind (flying fists) on a wet fingertip.
Hello again, hello. It's me (it's only me).

City bristlin' gloves today, handless,
cut off at the wrist. That's
supplication at best, at worst
the bait 'n grab of a supple leather

up-yours beneath her seat on the no. 18
uptown. As blue as that mitten
flash-frozen into prayer on this morning's
path. Yes, gloves gathering

in all the world's soiled places
where she's too long stared
herself down. Dear termagant,
like all collectors despairing

the end of the collection. Left
hand to match bleating calfskin
(no. 5 ½) or missing hand-
combed angora in damson

& plush. Brisk brisk, a walker
in the city stoops & strides, blush
blush away, glove clutched jittery
in hand, hand in hand.

That girl again, ho! A walker
in the city measures distance in feet,
defeats lengthening lamppost gaps,
width of a line scrawled

on a hasty page. As if walking
merely to conjugate the season's
crackling yellow declensions.
But winter now . . . winter

and the world funnels inwards,
declines, ah, elegant
within cagey astrakhan, between
closed lids, lips. Let's

catch her, moth-girl, against the lit
page, against flying leaves,
herself, selving, angular & awkward.
Girl with a name like a shrug,

a one-handed wave, terse
in the fly-leaf of some book
of posthumous queries. *How many
shoes did Dante wear out*

while writing the Commedia?
Breathes she a prayer (a curse)
cast visible in discrete
indiscreet puffs before sweeping

to heaven on an updraft. Then,
thighs she hard & trim
the street to her stride, alive
alive-o! A spasm of *agape*

gaping open in her throat
and morning
swinging sideways, flaring open
with her coat.

Like the last of the summer bees,
dazed, dashing for hothouse interiors,
bumbling the pockets of windbreakers,
satchel linings. This longing

for God that springs unholy water
gushing to the mouth as if
at the scent of meat grilling. Every year
'round this time summer tenses

past, a frantic bird flying
out of her mouth, flying south.
Well-cut eyes, curt temples: she loses
her temper more & moreish, allowing

thus everyone else to keep theirs.
Darkens, then, penitential violets
beneath her eyes. The people in this city
are like strike-anywhere matches,

blazing friendships on street corners,
in elevators. Ready to rub heads
with anyone, everyone, flaring briefly
in the dusk. Ah recompose

my disquiet. (Observe now
how she licks her fingers
between the pages of a book.) Look,
just as well, considering the darkness

falls each year not all of which
can extinguish the light
from a single cigarette, not
all the darkness. One day

mid-winters she a fist, pocket-
deep. Pulls out, frail & brown,
blown, the corpse of a thought
lost months ago

                    buzz

                          buzz

6

Comes the night and falls the snow.
That disproportion, snow,
resolved to perfect
the collapsing scaffold of winter.

Nothing else, not love or grief,
not anger or etiquette, Lordy, so
ex-*ces*-sive. That walker, mud-booted,
her hands, her cheeks, cold

as allegory as — as
that which escapes comparison, *ha!*
Yea though she walks,
cogitates she those honeycombed

lives. Lit windows, bent heads
absolving the dishes clean. Passes
the old city poet in his aerie,
dismantled this night by lust

or virtue, pacing his rooms, scribbling
poems to his circling
unsuitable self. (Burning the topless
towers of Ilium and so forth, muttering,

So? I misread the past. It was, after all,
a difficult book.) Come home, girl,
give us a kiss, do. Her fingers wet
and darkness falling

in decorous arches: tumbled, sprawling.

@

Hunched, hatching his little death
sits he, Brother Pig. That old poet all
squalorous and gone in the teeth
but the pitcher in him full or half

at least. A little leaking life, faith
& anti-faith hoarded equally, a loose
handful of words to turn the humming
world on its tilted ear, yas. Searches

for a word, a sentence takes off on its own,
joins someone else's poem.
So: walking girl leans windward, peels
nail polish in a thick rind, her long

nails clicking a tangerine rosary.
The old poet wonders what she looks like
(ah take this cup from my lips) does not
turn to belabour her points, charmed

by the coupla things already he knows.
As item: the unbroken
citrus curl. As item: a steady
devout click.

6

Last night, all polished hooves,
he cantered to a standstill.
Now he's woken, broken
on his rock. Seems the old eagle's

made a meal of him again.
Chopped liver & onions, ho,
a little sweetbread to leaven the pot,
light up the kidneys.

Scalpy old man! he chastises himself,
catching the whiff of mortality.
On another page a bird
imitates an alarm clock, the old poet

awakens in a magnesium flash
of dawn. A Sahara
of deft drift against the hourglass
renders thighs heavy, old pal,

as sand, and his breath stinks
of the lion house. Ah, all that falls
over the years away. What's left?
A day a day a day.

So, you think walking solves the world?
Cures what ails you? Nimbly she side-
steps his complex plaint, his inky
blue lines thrown out to reel

her in. The sky a soggy grey lung
overhead breathing *hoo*wah. Or no,
the winter sky snapping like bunting.
Either way comparisons evade

the subject, hasten to miss their
appointments. Lacking curves the way rivers
lack angles. His baited prose, I mean, his eye
tuned to the hazy blue frequencies

of distance. So? She is a walker in the city,
of young & brimming age, so
suffers the streets to move through her,
to move her. The foot a precise

approximation of length. Like poetic metre
or the distance at any one radius
between two radiant lovers. *Ah look what you
do done done to me!* whistles he

through the sugar cube in his teeth, that old
reprobate, his currentless
amblings all over this page, his mindful
heart, his capital F for art

(its vectoring flight). The seen frothing up
at the intersection of object & gaze,
the glaze, the light. *The seen*
leaking out of his eyes in cataracts.

⑨

Westward ho ho ho. Trudgy with weariness
off the gimlet shift and longing
for the vicious rounding of a little sleep.
But how to get home again, home-sweet

east-best and wee wee wee (all the way).
And she without her wings, without key
or compass or ruby mittens. She lost. Wan
& wondering, by the bus stop palely loitering.

Who owns this night the city?
Grain merchants, oilers and bankers, cutpurses,
rogues. Some slithy tove or other
in an office tower above Portage & Main.

The golden lad highballing his Legislature
or Worm the Conqueror? She walks
to disown. The Möbius spool
to spool of earth & sky, no joints showing:

unpremeditated snowing,
and then the lighting of the lamps.

Blinks the hazy orange eye
of the no. 18 in which an old party,
cable-knitted to a flecked rectitude,
faces inwards, profiling his spruce coin.

Above her dozy lapse,
the Heinz baby food baby
agape with joy. Mood Gush
to the Last Spoonerism!

Gathers the bus and rattles them
as stones into one pocket:
an old man, tired girl, that beamish tot
shiny as pate. Holy holy

at last, one family, at least
for another two stops.
Advert for Madonna & Child,
St. Joseph gazing benignly on

while the past tenses — perfects itself
in the future's radiant pigment.
What the city offers tentatively, tenderly,
late at night and far away from home:

the strangeness of kin, the body's thin
metal-fatigued chrome.

Fall, season of the *doppelgänger,* that unhoused
girl who straggles behind,
kicking leaves at his ankles. Wherever he goes
she follows, his canny adjective.

Give me a name, she begs, *and I'll leave.* Leaves,
autumn cut-outs
peel like decals from the illustrative elms.
Also, the matter of his sour

mood, snarling at smokers, coughers,
falterers between one step,
the next. And those who mumble
directions, palate banality, who knock

green apples against their teeth (*crisply*
on the bus) who fumble change
in the post office line. More or less,
these days, and then less and less.

A name, a name, she prods,
nose buried in tracts of fur
forty nylons once were slaughtered
to provide. Share they the wind,

the sky. Share they a fumbly history
of the knocks and falters a city delivers
in the course of a morning, say, skittering
on thin-skinned ice. Share they

wind-caper, sun-spin. Like him,
she is a walker in the city. Advance,
advance: they avoid as passersby avoid
each other's glance.

6

Season of packing up and digging in,
season of being done. *Her nifty scars,*
the silk-burns on her thighs, he writes.
(His notebook rustles like a Madonna

with a hundred white palms folded shut.)
Ah, but what to, what to do with her,
where to escort her, this walker?
He wants to write until she comes home to him

unfisting her small Modernist hands.
They share eyes, *unheimlich*
manoeuvre, blue snap of shadow across
alluvial snow. So —

so: a name like an indrawn breath, *cara*
mia. Easing her narrow shoulders
into the unused day, heave & hawk,
bulging to swallow a sip, a crumb.

A word smooth & oval as a pill — love,
say, or pain — gulped down
with the morning coffee. Give me
a name, she pants. Beside herself.

Cara mia, mea culpa. My darling, my fault.
(His fortunate importunate
fall.) Or consider static, a well-fed refrigerator
ruminating on its appetites.

Think of all those buzzing words
flashed down to a green asterisk,
centre of a blank afternoon: Mia, mine.
Centering the true of noon. As in:

whene'er in furs my Mia goes
then wakes she stars like footnotes
to the planets' discord. As in:
two walkers walking beneath high

crackling winds. As in: one following
or (to reverse the vice) one leading.
Caught like socks in the hot drum
of a dryer. Clinging statically,

ecstatically. Flashing blue into
true poetry. (And what about static
poems, hmm? Words that
crackle, words that cling?)

Fclix and Mia
walking the purr-air-ie
C. U. S. S. I. N. G.

wind cat's-pawed his jowl / her little cheek, pat pat

6

That dawning moment when the world,
framed in glass, enters the window pane.
Good morrow, waking soul! Mia wakes
hasty as a dreamer balked

by impossible metre. Nothing rhymes,
for example, orange. On subject of which
was colour named for fruit or fruit
for truth? A walker wakes, trailing

two fingers through wake
of sleep, aah . . . One of those
sudsy dreams drains thick & slow,
leaves lime stains and hard water

deposits on the inside of the mind.
Lint, lint . . . a day, a day,
one stride or breath too wide, too small.
Eventually all acorns fall, shaken free

from sky's blue tree. On subject of which
does left mean wrong? Can one begin
an autobiography without believing
the end of the story? On subject of which

what ebbs & flows from grief,
what wanes? And what
did dreamers dream before the invention
of tunnels and their trains?

The Beautiful Assassin:
A Poem Noir

Lo demás era muerte y sólo muerte
a las cinco de la tarde.

The rest was death, and death alone
at five in the afternoon.

— from "Lament for Ignacio Sanchez Mejias"
  by Federico García Lorca

7:05

The snowstorm begins at five past the hour,
always late always late,
like some huge harried white rabbit
clutching at its cuffs and moaning softly
into the wind.
Kulperstein lies potato-eyed in the dark, *lies*,
a man of resentment like Nietzsche was said to be
whenever his name was misspelled.
He is angry because of something — a bad review, a bad night,
a bad life. Now he is the carcass of a leopard
frozen in some high stony place.
Buried in all its heroic spots and unable to change them.
He is remembering his father,
who turned to salt from too much retrospection.
But his words held like water
contained unexpectedly in a sieve.

8:20

The girl — I'll call her Em — wakes with a start
as if an emery board run lightly over her life
has suddenly snagged on a silk thread.
Her lover stirs and reaches for her
and listen — it's as if she cracks into a hundred pieces
with rage and every jagged shard flings itself at his neck.
Instead she turns over on her back and practices her thought-balloons:
if I don't get there in time start without me
and *none for me thanks but please help yourself.*
At twelve years old, good manners
descended upon her like a *deus ex machina.*
Now she is a thin gruel of early winter on the ground.
Above her, her lover labours on.
Every breath cracks like knuckles.

9-ish

The old poet dozes, wakes, shakes
the sealing wax from his ears,
loosens his bonds and steps away from his place at the mast.
Damn those sirens! Caterwauling all night long!
I am a very old ghost, he thinks to himself,
with nothing but time on my hands and melancholy feet.
It is true, his feet suffer from cafard.
And why? Because of fallen arches and memory.
Here comes a procession of his ex-lovers leaving
phosphorous on his pillow and malice that shines in the dark.
Yes, the lovers are angry today and the sea is as heavy as wet hair.
Cafard! they cry, before he can replace the sealing wax.
It is a trident word and it pins him to the mast in tatters.
Melancholic! Hypocrite! Cockroach!
Ah, poor feet, the distances you have to travel to die.
Miles, days, years into the past
tense and trembling.

10:10

The lover has unbelted his sex and laid it like a scabbard
on the breakfast table.
Too much, too much, Em murmurs,
trying to turn herself back into a photograph, a mirror,
a small effigy of the Virgin delicately grooming her hair
and coughing up babies.
Outside, ambulances belch through the streets
as if digesting their cargoes.
Inside, clocks hold up cupped hands,
words grow teeth, light pours from his ears.
Ho! he shouts and then — but much later — *Ha!*
What is that sound? That nylon squeak of snow underfoot?
It is the sound of Em making good her escape,
it is the old cut-rate angel folding her over his arm
like clean laundry.

Elevenses

Kulperstein is weary of jamming his toast and bloodying his Marys.
La chair est triste, hélas! et j'ai lu tous les livres.
His head is enormous, a pumpkin all lit up, and his tongue
is a tiny wick of rage guttering in the well of his mouth.
       Rum, that.
He is practicing his sums by counting all the world's stories
but finds there are still only two: a lover runs waving
to his beloved on a train.
In the first story he almost catches up, in the second he almost does not.
Or no, three. There's the one about the stranger who comes to town.
Kulperstein remembers when the world was still in black & white stock
and folks were shiny, as if polished up
by a little salt & pessimism. *Son,* says his father,
bursting suddenly through the saloon doors,
a mirage is only an argument that looks the same
from all points of view.

The Long Dash

Em, the librarian, is listening to the books humming on their shelves.
They are reading themselves between closed covers
with a sound like power lines at high voltage.
These books are ready to kill; don't open them,
or do — it's up to you, it always was. Em recalls that first
electric apple plucked from the tree —
a jolt, a buzz,
the lights in the public library dimming momentarily.
Suddenly the horizon astonishes by emitting a loud gong.
Is this the signal to arrange all her pretty breasts in a row
and divide her teeth evenly between two halves of a smile?
Now words are hissing from pages, whizzing around the room
as if to say *squeeze of lemon lick of salt open wound wound wound.*
Em, ever obedient, tries to scoop them up
and stuff them back into their mackintoshes.
Ho! good luck, Em (hastily she pockets *snub-nosed revolver*)
good luck with all that shelving.

1:25

Same old used to be, thinks the old poet,
same old window, sky, soul hanging like a dust mote in the.
Same stale angel-smell in the morning, sulphur and singed feathers.
Same fleas plucked from beneath wings,
flicked across the room by a crooked yellow forefinger.
Somewhere in the city, a hole the size of his death has been prepared.
Now it only remains to knock him in.
Ho hum! old poet snaps his eyes and his hat brim, his beak, and away
he goes, a zealot for bad causes.
Walking turns the future into a list of fragile nouns: what may be
broken. Day, eggs, hearts, horses.
Bones, silence, glass, rhythm.
Shoes broken in, light broken through, prisoners
out. That old stink-angel of history, similarly out.
Cupboards and ancient categories. Both out.
Old poet breathes in, thawing winter
with each zinc white breath, out.

Pas de Deux

In the bar called Naked Lunch the girls are dancing with their poles
as if they are the only poles in the world, the poles before whom
all other poles must bow down.
The one called Em shines like eggplant tossed in olive oil
but even men who are not vegetarians want to eat her.
In Mr. Manet's painting of a naked lunch there are no poles
but there are men struck rigid with the effort of averting their allegory.
Oef! they are saying, *the brisk breezes of Argenteuil give one an appetite!*
while Victorine parts their hunger with her stare.
For, alas, Mr. Manet has provided little in the way of a picnic lunch.
Is this a painting about propriety or a paltry meal,
the difficulty of naming one or the other being the difference
between what is naked and what is nude?
Let's split a leaf salad, says Mr. Manet to the old poet in the bar
where the girls are divided down the middle of the afternoon
by their vertical sufficiency.

3:45

A drowning man is not troubled by rain,
goes a particularly unwise Persian proverb.
Kulperstein assumes the Persians were a landlocked people (wrong)
who lived under perpetual drought knowing
nothing of rain (wrong again)
or were improbable stoics (wrong wrong).
It is late in the afternoon and Kulperstein tramples the long shadow
of his death as it slants across drifting snow.
But his feet hurt and his palms itch and his liver is a tight fit
and his five o'clock shadow is early again.
Yes, the rain, the rain!
Oh Kulperstein, you old voluptuary of pain, what can you tell us
about the chilly instructiveness of suffering?
Dunno, he mutters, suddenly shy. *Unless —*
have you heard the one about the origin of tears?
Only ten percent are caused by grief.
All the rest are onions and accident, ole pal,
a yawn, a chuckle, a poke in the eye.

4:59

For whoever proceeds on his own path meets nobody,
writes Nietzsche in a late preface to a work much less beautiful
than what precedes it.
He is living in Ruta, near Genoa, in the autumn of 1886.
Hot winds bearing the scent of nuts & quince, smoke from steamers
in the nearby port, blow through the preface.
This pilgrim with eyes shuddering like knives thrown at the horizon.
. . . *meets nobody,* reads Em,
who has met many people, many,
before coming to this white-shaped thought.
This path, this page.
She has a contract to fulfill, she has a *snub-nosed revolver*
in the pocket of her *trench coat.*
She slants into the wind like handwriting,
holding the book before her face as a disguise.

:

The world has begun to blur at the edges (it always happens).
First the words disappear from the page, then the expressions
on the faces of passersby.
Soon all the people resemble clocks without hands.
What time is it?
In the distance one can hear the footsteps of the old poet
proceeding on his solitary path.
But hark! Someone is coming towards him.
A man with a great mirror lodged in his brain.
Guten Tag und wie geht es Ihnen?
Em closes her book, checks her sightlines.
What time— His eyes
swivel back, burn
through his skull. Stink like cordite.

6:30

No time! thinks Em, hurrying home through the digital snow.
She has been *unavoidably delayed*,
time, spliced with its interruption,
jerking through the day's cranky shutter.
And now there is none of it,
although a blizzard of random numbers keeps popping up
above the heads of passersby.
4:59! 8:20! 1:25!
O tempora! worries Em, thinking of the intemperate lover,
if I don't get there in time start without me.
 She no longer resembles her photograph
and all the mirrors have slammed shut.
But her feet in their winter boots
shine with phosphorous, track
salt water and wake and bright murderous krill
all the way home.

7:04

Kulperstein lies on his back inside his chalk outline, *lies.*

Hangnail moon, whitlow moon, crooked moon. Dark.
All the people in the city exhale at once,
standing in the street with their eyes shut.
Sleepwalkers, can you, can you thaw
the frozen chuck of winter
shoved in the back of the freezer?
Nope.
Better wait for spring runoff, the bloom of tender meat.

Kulperstein was dying again and again.
He was damn good at it but wouldn't quit until he found
the perfect metaphor.
Your stone ball, Father, he hazarded. *Your stone joke, bus, glance.*
These were things that could be thrown and when thrown, caught
or missed. Kulperstein was always missing his father
with inches to spare.
They were two wishbones broken in exactly the same place.

Being Dead

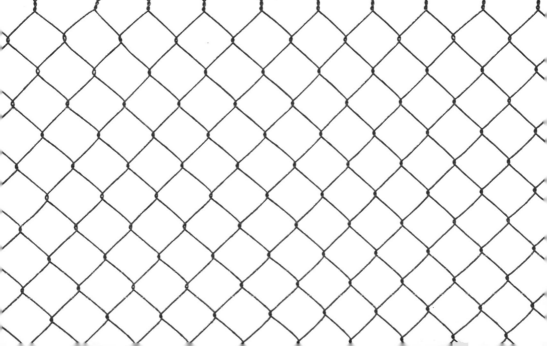

Forgive me for what I'm telling you;
Quietly, quietly read it back to me.

— from Posthumous Poems in *Selected Poems*
  by Osip Mandelstam

His Eyes

But he hasn't opened them once
since he died, poor lad.
Beneath twitching lids they spin
like hot brown pennies.
Heads or tails, dear fellow? Your game.
The cursive rain slants down,
hissing, and the geese, hissing,
slant cursing against the moon.
Black spots across a blank eye.

His Feet

Oh let me sing to you of shoes, pilgrim!
and slowness.
Besides, we are friends of the lento, says Nietzsche,
tapping him with the heel of his argument.
Yes, like that. Tap tap
(a leisurely proposition).
It seems that when his walking shoes were unearthed
they were found to be empty of feet.
Somebody has robbed a grave or a syllogism,
ambling from the general to the particular as if to say,
Count to infinity by tens
and see if you get there any quicker.

His Peach

What breaks, what is broken?

This story of his death
that takes the imprint of fingers
like a bruised fruit.

What is fleeting, what endures, and what
is unendurable?

A body packed in its own juices,
fermenting, beginning
to run.

His "Heart"

A fist clutching at the earth.
Old cockney Art dropping his *H*s again.
Four red rooms to live inside.
The rhythm section.
What country & western songs have 16 different names for
(though they all sound the same).
Bit of beef boiling in the ground.
Piece of red rag to a bull.
Angle of the angel at noon (no shadows).
Not smash on rock, not pant in flame,
not trample under His hard foot
and break and break and break.

His Heart Redux

The wet snout.
The dry bone.
(The space between.)
Location of three things not easily seen in the dark (knife, wolf, hunger).
The hole in the poem where blood pulses through.
(Wolf balances on hunger's knife, pushes her snout into a hole.)
Words like muscles push push.
(*Pumps* her snout into, *lunges* the poem between.)
Dawn, weather, bones (sympathetic list of things easily broken).
Knife throws itself into the wolf called Hunger. Her heart.

His Rot

And death flowing like honey
from a broken honeycomb,
as if some clumsy-thumbed boy
reaching up into the hive
(sun-dazzled, distracted by summer's
dark mortal hum)
has poked his finger
through the cell walls
to what also leaks
stickiness.
All day the boy
puts his finger to his nose,
sniffs dreamily, puzzled
by the ripe ochre stink.

His Yeast

We buried him carefully, a new loaf
proving beneath damp cloth
then rising swiftly in a hot oven.
Smell of beer and good cheer.
Tousled elms let fall their delicate green
canker worms as we left the cemetery,
recalling the bright green mohair sweater
that would soon wrap him in its arms.

His Hands

Dead three days and already they've begun to grow!
Now they are as swollen as white opera gloves
or the hands of a boy murderer who has slain a giant
and been turned to stone with incredulity.
Oh Donatello, and you too Giambologna,
and you most of all, Michelangelo, who understands
that hands are verbs in the body's hard marble
sentence.
Somewhere on a windy plain in Judah
the son of Jesse the Bethlehemite
kneels to search for five plausible stones,
smoothing his crisp white decorum over his knuckles
as if to say, *Hands! how far we have come
from first plantings.*

His, His

humours blowing through him, black bile
stopping the valves of his great heart's great
organ and melancholy draining in & out,
in & out, like blood in an aortal cavity.
                                  And, and grief,
yes, and grief's attributes: rain, teeth,
cat, zipper, thorn, morning, all snagging
on skin. As for him his, his
flesh grows daily looser, flakes away
from the bone.
                                  Until death
that old fork, worn tarnished & thin,
pitches him in.

His Spring

Spring knuckles him awake from the long bear-fat sleep.
Eee-oh, ole pal, turn over!
Clock-faced and slightly ticking, he opens an eye
on the most rickety, unsprung, rusty old Spring
in the history of the world,
poking its broken bedsprings from the soil,
all loose teeth and cut wrists.
The tulip bulbs have been buried alive,
someone has trimmed the daffodil wicks
and the bees have swarmed his resistance.
All month the rain gibbers down, a sour rain
like turned milk or the face of the woman
who has downed it straight from the carton,
standing halfway into the fridge, her throat eerily lit
in the dark kitchen. And Spring,
Spring knuckles him awake to fields ploughed
with dead mice, dead clocks, all the dead darlings
sprouting swift green shoots from their eyeholes.

His Ribcage

A hull rocking on some warm, dark
underground current, sliding
through summer's deep crevices.
Give me a minute and I'll count to sixty
with the broad Mississippi flowing between
seconds like milestones on the riverbank.

His Tongue

The irises blurt from his mouth in the spring,
their quick purple darts at translation
(of air into green and green into lung and concertina
and umbrella) the whole breathing world opening & shutting
in mad zipperish gaiety: *parapluie, parapluie!*

Little purple flames billow from his mouth:
the dragon lies underground, gnawing his terror
and practicing his courtly love sonnets.
With every knight that burns & swoons,
he clutches at his bulbous testicles *très fort.*

Out of his mouth flops a long purple insole
from an old boot that has been dragging its feet
for many years. And boot has come too far,
chattering about the road, the pace, the clipped
horizon. Oh boot, boot, hold your tongue, do!

His Brain

Brain haiku dices
face thin-sliced like onion
behind chicken mind.

Brain like alfalfa
peaks early then goes to seed.
Birds eat metaphor.

Steamed cauliflower,
sprinkled salt, sprinkled lostness.
Too much *salt*, I think.

His Soul

Summer arrives with the clash of dragonfly wings
skimming the sun's taut eye.
A bird cocks its head, ducks once, pours itself
in song like water out. Even the worm
has turned.
Oh ho, worm has made a nest of him
and laid her eggs.
Now all is new life, warm & teeming.
And the colours are like the soul's journey
through oil paint: heart's blood, gall, green
as goose liver, tangle of varicose blue, and kidneys
all lit up like a couple of kitchen bulbs
hanging above a summer porch at dusk.

Posthumous:
A Chapbook

Publisher 's Note

The poet Felix Kaye, as many people know, died last year in the middle of a poem. This is not to say that he was writing a poem when he died, but that he was living it. Somehow he had gotten himself right in between the lines and it killed him. Art killed him.

　　Requiescat in pace.

　　It is our great privilege to publish as a chapbook, the handful of poems left with his editor when he died. *The Book of Imaginary Fathers* was his working title and, given the importance of the father as subject and symbol in his poetry, we can think of no better. Our thanks are due to his amanuensis, Ms. Em Cook, whose assistance with the selection and assembly of the posthumous material has been invaluable.

A Note on Aliases

The poet F. Kulperstein who inhabits the poetry of Felix Kaye with such persistence is either a real person or a fictional poet. Little is known about him except that he lived in a mid-sized city in the centre of North America around the middle of the last century. He was comically attracted by middles, says Kaye, his alter ego; his trajectory was centrifugal and his disposition equatorial.

　　His best known book, *Loitering With Intent*, was published the year of Kaye's tragic death but was accompanied by no author appearances, readings or signings. Nothing has been heard from him since, although a curious public waits.

The Book of Imaginary Fathers

(Incomplete)

by Felix Kaye

God Father

A harlequin argument for the existence of God.
Much patched in patterns of blindness and its dark opposite,
insight.
For what would freedom be were the dead not also liberated?
At least the ones who live within us.
(Perhaps there are no others?)
In our disgraces dwell also our graces.

Electricity Father

"Preserved like a moth in a light bulb."
But what?
The soul's hunger for immolation, the heart's longing that burns dust
from filament, the, the tremulous fluttering of *the good?*
Felix, lad, change the porch light, I can hardly —
Moon's half full tonight, he observes.
But then I've always been an incurable optimist.
And revelation?
Hmm. A narrowing of self, an arrowing.
Not open or shut, but slightly ajar.
Horizons burning near & far, his scattering eye
and the years going the way of all yearning.

Gift Horse Father (1)

Here, said the old man,
his *soi-disant* father,
handing him
a stone glove.

Gift Horse Father (2)

Here, said the old man, his father many times removed
handing him a page flowing white as milk
poured into milk.
Dissolve a little water
into water.
Or substitute, he relented on his deathbed,
oil for one measure water.
Ten stark half moons rose from his nail beds
and his pupils flexed, *twang*, to shutter speed.
Here, said the old man, cuffing his son's vagrant wrist.
Come closer, look harder.
In his father's eyes, two trees flashed sunlight,
burst out of their leaves.
Here, said the old man, drawing his son
ever closer
to his own green fracture.

Vowel Father

He has lived through so many returns, eyes reddening
from the slight friction of seeing.
His family sits around the table, nibbling on jellied calf.
Overhead an airplane curtly flaps its wings.
He returns home at last, *Knock knock!*
Who's there? calls the good rabbi, biting
into a vowel round as an onion.
Prodigal sunlight enters to illuminate
a little heap of shoes and teeth, eyeglasses
milky as cataracts.
High-ho, a plane banks steeply, spirals down
into the middle of the twentieth century.
Me who? The old man rises from the wreckage
and brushes off his gabardine.
Sets his ringlets to rights and braids up his fringes.

Gift Horse Father (3)

Here, said the old man, his far & away ever father,
handing him a stone door.
Open the door, on a table, open a drawer, lies a book.
(Or a face or a drawbridge, a forest, a hand.)
What may be opened and when opened
slammed shut.
(Mouth, mind, oven, history.)
Knock knock, said the old man, rapping briskly
on his stone joke.

Our Father

Oh father with your face like a fist in a pocket
and that habit of kicking your shadow downstairs
as if to say, *Stop following me, lazybones!*
Legs so short these days they barely reach the ground,
and only just your shoes.
Epaulettes can't restrain you and buttons spray from you
with each deep breath.
A drum, a dog, an argument, you taught us,
are three things that can be beaten.
A child in its eggshell skin.
Your conscience afterwards, partly.
But you have not lost your hospitality, dear one,
as you reach into the freezer for the ice tray.
And all the little cubes of ice,
with just one twist from your fingers,
crack like teeth.

Adam Father

He wakes up naked and drunk as a bear
on sun-fermented garbage.
Hungover and queasy and riled up by bees.
Nothing going well today, he moans,
life being short and the craft, ah, long.
Still, might as well take a stab at it,
lording it over misrule and tending the shame
that transforms a garden into Genesis.

So there he goes, stalking through the world
on his back legs, pelting down half-eaten words
from a great height.
Whatever he touches shrieks and bellows or writhes
like the alphabet.
A is for Crocodile, he croaks,
dashing through the Everglades. See you later!
And B is for the Wasp that stings him and C —
C is for the wide blue Ocean
in which he nearly drowns.

But nothing can drown him, our Adam
whose resolution is steadfast
and breezy at last, and buoyant
as a stone boat.

Impatient Father

The tree made a nest and sang, put out blossoms
then fruit then pies & crumbles,
caught kites in its arms, paper bags, a kitten.
Where where where? sang the wind, a cappella,
and Eve looked everywhere,
but the search for apples was fruitless.
Drop everything! went the singing telegram.
Drop everything and hurry to the Gate
where your Emperor waits for you
with flowers in his beard.

Weary Father

This city in which you have knocked about
like an old pipe all these years,
knocked yourself out, against
(elbows, knees)
broken and passively tense.
Wondering, is love focus or blur?
Is lust monkey or bird? And can
a little sweetness be pressed
out of the hard & meagre years?
Some questions snag like metal teeth
on your windbreaker.
Some questions stop and sway on every floor,
like crowded elevators.
A year is not an orange, you tell yourself,
watching from over the rim of your coffee
as the sun rises and hangs in the sky,
round & juicy.

Dear Father

You say that bird outside your window
keeps imitating an alarm clock
and waking you up in the middle of the night?
Must work the fat off your nerves all right.
And while we're on the subject of nerve,
here's how to stop the onions from bullying you:
Peel under running water.
Hold a kitchen match between your teeth.
Salt your cutting board.
Or lightly pepper your fancy.
Don't worry, it's vegetables not grief,
it always was. Just wait it out
is what you taught me: birds die
or run out of batteries at least, or learn
other mimicries. A bottle of gin, perhaps,
clouding over gently in the freezer
of your good regard.

                    Hope so,
                        Your son.

Writing Father

With your writer's rolling eyeball
clicking off one horizon or another,
and your bold & swarmy breath
huffing in my ear, you taught me
molecular disdain
for every creature overflowing
the sloppy little Petri dish
of its soul.
Rainwater dripping through rock
and saxifrage bursting out of it
were your models.
No Pity was the deal you struck
with God and me, the deal I keep
when you lope from the thickets
of your impenetrable verse
into the flaring headlights
of a bad driver, a good reader.

Appendix A

The Keyhole Poems

Mia dresses hastily, her body a pale
hyphen between "wakes" and "woken,"
between awaken and broken, between
two kinds of definition, both hard

of hearing, between legs and lips (a gush,
a yawn) between days, winter's
perfect spacing narrowing at the seams.
Between blindness, insight, and outside,

vertical blinds and the new day, out of true,
crowding up against. A perfect moment
to the left and right of which are
inadequate moments. As when winter's

thinnest bear lumbers *à bout de souffle*
from her lair. Locking the front door,
rehearsing the permissible traction
in the word *fall*. (Actually, keys are only

symptoms, *Monsieur*.) Mia, mine own.
Angular bones, coupla wire coat hangers
poking skittishly beneath rare skin. Skins.
To fall: asleep, in love, from grace. Into

reverie. Away from the bone. Or,
to earth. As in: she dropped her handkerchief
but retained her faculties.
Night and snow, leaves, rain, and tears,

if one is not particular, fall, all down.
Ashes, ashes. Blood, of course (murderously)
flies upward. Even a nosebleed
for which one may procure a key,

metal-cold, to lock up the sinuses.

6

Except for this skin and how she lives in it,
chooses to live, I should say, and not
without grace. Ha!
But she knows her heels and how to dig in.

The sky has the tone of a flute today,
wayward, with a top note of — hmm . . .
metal, breath, Bach. Is the past a key
worn thin with use?

Well-cut eyes, a cropped mouth,
a certain, hem hem, prune & prisms
elocution. O lemmings, *lemmings!*
Look before you leap, *do!* But her skin

shimmers, pelts light. A smile
analogous to vanished beauty and so on.
Love, of course, & grief, grace, implausible
chaste virtue, manners and, yes, the acrylic

sheen of good intentions.

6

There goes old poet, bestriding
the world, Struwwelpeter hair all
on end in his black & blue polka
dotage. There he goes, gulping

wine the colour of that drunken
Homeric sea. *Opa opa!*
His soul hauled like a tumbled
sweater from the dryer, inside out,

sleeves unravelling. *Hey aren't you*
glad you're not an orange?
Old poet with his do or dare, his *chair*
est triste, la chair la chair. Hélas!

Begin again: *Knock knock, who's there?*
Old poet turns himself into a stiletto
and throws himself at the keyhole.
And all the lovely women

turn around, turn as one
and tumble in their locks.

Through the Keyhole

She shrugs coat, sweater, blouse,
her skin. Emerges tender as a peeled
grape, green irises shining
through transparent lids. Settle down,

settle down, fold yourself against the spine!
She opens the book to spray & squall,
a poem's sea breeze bearing all
before, behind, aloft, adrift (some Symbolist

sea tilting its faceted waves
like cursive letters on the page).
Perdus, sans mâts, sans mâts . . .
There is nothing to hold onto anymore,

and when she reads, her fingers
are wet. The book flutters thin, thinner
in her hands while she *mmm* fattens.
Words settle like sediment, bottom-

heavy as pear, lamplight shining
in her hair.
Who are you, luminous one?
Who are you, well-mannered terror?

A woman bends like a question mark
over the astonishment of her page.

Appendix B

Follow Me

Mandelstam measures the *Commedia*
in feet. Gradual cantos laid end
on end to reach God or the devil.
How many inches in a foot? How many

fingers on one hand clapping
out the intervals between key changes,
the spaces between stairs, stars?
Cagily done, Signor Alighieri!

Vagabonding through the middle of your
dark wood. Pacing out the distance
between Heaven & Hell
in footsteps, in worn out soles, tongues

flapping. In trochee of discarded shoes.
Such poems can only be written
while wandering away from some
well-heeled city. Ah grindstone & nose,

shoulder, wheel, the foot, the foot
beating out time's clompy two-step
so fast the nouns blurred as we passed
and events swiftly verbed themselves

the better to keep pace. *Love is all
bugger all*, whistles Mandelstam
(another exile) and Kulperstein,
silent as toes

in felt slippers, pads after.

Chest jarred, his shins splinting,
Signor Alighieri paces out his en
jambments. Hind legs pinching,
stomach taut with puckered green olives

stolen from the trees near Ravenna
whose knowledge of good & evil
is partial at best, the poet Mandelstam
follows in his footsteps.

Breathes in fumy diesel, sharp
acceleration of dust. The long, late
Mezzogiorno decline. Declensions
various: it is or was always dusk / soon,

soon, all will be dust. Thoughts so full tonight
he carries them carefully, a brimming cup
in both hands. Heavy as metaphor
or what the metaphor can't carry. Ha!

For what seems like months,
even *weeks*, the past lengthens behind him,
until every day is a day
that has come undone at the seams

like a badly run-up canto.

Last Poems

(from *Loitering With Intent* by F. Kulperstein)

Sleepwalking

Sleepwalkers awake! stumbling about
with your eyes burning slow holes
in the insides of your minds for words
in the shape of birds to flap through.

And your great ropes of keys
swinging from your necks. So many keys,
which in this city can be exchanged
for goods & services, even food,

even love. Well keys, you know,
are hard & cold, and stick
to the tongue on winter nights.
They are the iron syllables

that open the locked rooms
of the past.
Sleepwalkers, if you shuffle about
long enough are you bound

to come at last to a familiar place,
a place you've lived before,
a street name that opens tiny locks
all over the skin? Knock twice

and ask for him, that young boy
who comes to the door of — McMillan Ave.
and stands there in his striped pajamas,
rubbing the birds out of his eyes.

Girl, Walking

              Ah you, bright you,
breaking day open like a dry loaf
and setting off through the billowing sky
that wafts across your mind

like shantung curtains. Girl,
you have cured my mournfulness
the way you bounce through the rubber museum
of all my enterprise. For example:

your lips are worn thin from too many
insincere kisses, and yet
they are still your lips — unmistakable!
They are not (forgive me) poetic lips or lips

in danger of creating an insubordinate
lineage among poets who keep quoting
one another *like ducks* on the subject
of plagiarism: quack quack quack!

But for all that, girl, yes *you* —
you have brightened
my blue period and what has been slammed
most recently shut.

              Ah you, bright you,
with your unlatched laughter
and love contagious as yawning,
you are why all my locks tumble

and what springs open
this weary heart of mine.

Daybreak

So, old ghost, old familiar,
your crests all fallen
and your red-eyed insomniac cigarette
making circles in the dark

as you line up the sheep
and all their hard-working
sleepless nights. Counting counting.
Like fat white questions jumping over a gate!

How may we learn that death
awaits us? What is hunger?
And what happens to that girl, that walker,
when the poem is finished?

Well, old ghost, old familiar,
we might never know, or know only
the fade to white, the turned page.
And somewhere a screen door swings,

latched, unlatched,
all night long. As for you,
huddled in your loose skin
all cowled about the neck

and still counting, counting
all that you have lost: gloves,
sleep, keys, temper, time . . .
And somewhere

a dusty bulb still hangs
above a porch
and lights up a little falling circle
of the fallen world.

A Pact

Gentle reader, come with me
into my brown study, my wood
of shapely green thoughts,
where we will all recover

from childhood and climb trees
in order to gain perspective!
Oh, please come,
don't let me have this *folie à deux*

alone. Let us comfort one another
when the dead swiftly turn ghost
and chase each other,
striking matches on their finger bones.

Gentle reader, I imagine you
shining in the light
of an open book, yes, and the years
turning over in you like pages.

This page was once a leaf,
you urge gently. Urgently.
This page was a leaf once,
this book a tree.

Let us go then, gentle one, you and I,
into this wood of our shared delusion,
where leaves glisten like drops
of green arterial blood.

Acknowledgements

Earlier versions of some of these poems have appeared in *Border Crossings*, *CV2*, *Grain Magazine*, *enRoute Magazine*, *Prairie Fire* and *The Winnipeg Review* as well as the anthologies *A/Cross Sections*, edited by Andris Taskans and Katherine Bitney and *Best Canadian Poetry in English 2008*, edited by Stephanie Bolster. My appreciation to the editors. "A Walker in the City" was performed on *Between the Covers*, CBC Radio One. In the fall and winter of 2008 the poem on page 12 was included on a bus card that appeared on various city buses as part of the Poetry in Motion initiative. I'd especially like to thank the amiable bus drivers of routes 61 and the good old 18 Riverbend for transporting poetry through the byways of our city.

The poem alluded to on pages 33, 80 and 81 is "Brise Marine" by Stéphane Mallarmé. I have also made free, on page 38, with the preface to Nietzsche's *Daybreak*.

Grateful thanks to the Canada Council, the Manitoba Arts Council, and the Winnipeg Arts Council for graciously providing me with time to complete this collection and to The Centre for Creative Writing and Oral Culture at the University of Manitoba for a winter residency and a lively community with which to share it.

For stern encouragement when it was needed and gentle criticism where it was deserved, much gratitude to Barry Dempster, Catherine Hunter, Mary di Michele and the members of the April 2010 master class. For their support of poetry and their general excellence, hosannas to Alayna Munce, Cheryl Dipede, Kitty Lewis, Alan Siu and the splendid crew at Brick Books and a loud hurrah to Stan Dragland, wise editor and good friend.

And thank you to Mark Libin — gentle reader, gentleman — for everything.

Biographical Note

A Walker in the City is Méira Cook's third book of poetry with Brick Books. The opening poem of this collection won first place in the 2006 CBC Literary Awards, and poems in this series were selected as part of the Poetry in Motion initiative, allowing poetry to circulate through the streets on city buses.

She lives, writes, and walks in Winnipeg.